Shaquille O'Neal

by A. R. Schaefer

Reading Consultant:
Dr. Robert Miller
Professor of Special Education
Minnesota State University, Mankato

CAPSTONE
HIGH-INTEREST
BOOKS

an imprint of Capstone Press
Mankato, Minnesota

Capstone High-Interest Books are published by Capstone Press
151 Good Counsel Drive, P.O. Box 669, Mankato, Minnesota 56002
http://www.capstone-press.com

Library of Congress Cataloging-in-Publication Data
Schaefer, A. R. (Adam Richard), 1976–
    Shaquille O'Neal/by A.R. Schaefer.
    p. cm.—(Sports heroes)
    Summary: Examines the life and basketball career of the Los Angeles Lakers
"big man" who led his team to two consecutive NBA championships in 2000 and 2001.
    Includes bibliographical references (p. 45) and index.
    ISBN 0-7368-1297-0 (hardcover)
    1. O'Neal, Shaquille—Juvenile literature. 2. Basketball players—United States—
Biography—Juvenile literature. [1. O'Neal, Shaquille. 2. Basketball players. 3. African
Americans—Biography.] I. Title. II. Sports heroes (Mankato, Minn.)
GV884.O46 S35 2003
796.323'092—dc21   2001008187

Editorial Credits
Matt Doeden, editor; Karen Risch, product planning editor; Timothy Halldin, series designer;
    Gene Bentdahl, book designer and illustrator; Jo Miller, photo researcher

Photo Credits
AFP/CORBIS, 4, 7, 35, 36
Ales Fevzer/CORBIS, 33
Brian Drake/SportsChrome-USA, 14, 26, 29
Brian Spurlock/SportsChrome-USA, cover, 10, 38, 42
David L. Johnson, SportsChrome-USA, 18, 23
Duomo/CORBIS, 17
Maria D. Cerda/Zuma/Timepix, 41
Michael Zito/SportsChrome-USA, 9, 20
Reuters NewMedia, Inc./CORBIS, 24
SportsChrome-USA, 12, 30

1 2 3 4 5 6 07 06 05 04 03 02

Table of Contents

CHAPTER 1

Most Valuable Player

On June 8, 2001, the Los Angeles Lakers were playing the Philadelphia 76ers in Game 2 of the NBA Finals. The 76ers had already won the first game of the series.

Shaquille O'Neal stepped onto the court for the Lakers. Shaq had already been named the NBA's Most Valuable Player (MVP). Shaq also wanted to prove that he could lead the Lakers to victory.

The 76ers began the game well. In the second quarter, they held a 40-33 lead. But

---

In 2001, Shaq led the Lakers to the NBA Finals.

Shaq then scored 10 points in four minutes of play. He also grabbed several rebounds and blocked shots on the defensive end. Suddenly, the Lakers held a 45-43 lead.

Shaq continued to play well in the second half. He finished the game with 28 points, 20 rebounds, nine assists, and eight blocked shots. Shaq's great performance helped the Lakers to a 98-89 win.

The Lakers went on to win the next three games. They were the NBA champions for the second year in a row. During the five games, Shaq averaged 33 points and almost 16 rebounds per game. He also was named NBA Finals MVP for the second year in a row.

About Shaquille O'Neal

Shaquille O'Neal is the starting center for the Los Angeles Lakers. He has played for the Lakers since 1996. Before that, he played for the Orlando Magic.

Shaq was named MVP of the 2001 NBA Finals.

Shaq is 7 feet, 1 inch (216 centimeters) tall and weighs 315 pounds (143 kilograms). He is one of the biggest players in the NBA. His size and skills make him one of the most dominant players in NBA history.

Basketball is not Shaq's only talent. He also enjoys acting. He has starred in several movies, including *Blue Chips* and *Kazaam*. He often appears in advertisements for products that he endorses. Shaq also has recorded several rap music albums.

CAREER STATISTICS

Shaquille O'Neal

NBA Per-Game Statistics

Year	Team	FG%	Pts	Reb	Ast	Blk
92–93	ORL	.562	23.4	13.9	1.9	3.53
93–94	ORL	.599	29.3	13.2	2.4	2.85
94–95	ORL	.583	29.3	11.4	2.7	2.43
95–96	ORL	.573	26.6	11.0	2.9	2.13
96–97	LAL	.557	26.2	12.5	3.1	2.88
97–98	LAL	.584	28.3	11.4	2.4	2.40
98–99	LAL	.576	26.3	10.7	2.3	1.67
99–00	LAL	.574	29.7	13.6	3.8	3.03
00–01	LAL	.572	28.7	12.7	3.7	2.76
01–02	LAL	.579	27.2	10.7	3.0	2.04
Career		.577	27.6	12.3	2.8	2.63

CHAPTER 2

The Early Years

Shaq was born March 6, 1972, in Newark, New Jersey. His mother is Lucille O'Neal. Lucille chose the name "Shaquille" because it means "little warrior" in the Arabic language.

When Shaq was two, Lucille married Philip Harrison. Harrison was not Shaq's biological father. But Shaq always called Philip his "real dad." Shaq also has two younger sisters named Lateefah and Ayesha and a younger brother named Jamal.

Shaq was born March 6, 1972.

A HERO'S HERO

Julius Erving (Dr. J)

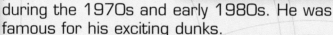

Shaq watched many basketball players as he grew up. One of his favorites was Julius Erving. Erving's nickname was "Dr. J."

Erving was one of the biggest stars in professional basketball during the 1970s and early 1980s. He was famous for his exciting dunks.

Erving played college basketball at the University of Massachusetts. In 1972, he left school to join the Virginia Squires of the American Basketball Association (ABA).

Erving played for the Squires for two years. He then joined the New York Nets for three years. He led the Nets to ABA titles in 1974 and 1976. He was named the league's MVP in each of his three seasons with the Nets.

In 1976, the ABA merged with the NBA. Erving joined the Philadelphia 76ers. He won the NBA MVP award in 1981 and led the 76ers to an NBA title in 1983.

Erving retired in 1987. He was elected to basketball's Hall of Fame in 1993.

On the Move

Philip was in the U.S. Army. The family moved often. Shaq lived in places such as Germany, Georgia, and New Jersey.

Shaq was very large for his age. At 4, he was already 3 feet, 10 inches (117 centimeters) tall. By age 12, he was nearly 6 feet (183 centimeters) tall. People sometimes thought that Shaq was older than he really was. The other children teased him. They said he must have failed several grades in school. But Shaq actually began school a year early. He was younger than most of his classmates.

As a child, Shaq wanted to be an actor or a dancer. He was not interested in basketball. But he quickly learned that his size and strength were a big advantage in basketball. He became more interested in the sport.

In 1985, Philip and the family returned to Germany. Shaq was 13. He was already 6 feet, 8 inches (203 centimeters) tall. He quickly became one of the best young basketball players in Germany. But people continued to accuse him of lying about his age.

Shaq hoped that his basketball skills would allow him to play in the NBA.

Life in Germany

Coach Dale Brown from Louisiana State University (LSU) once came to the army base to give a basketball clinic. Shaq was excited to show his skills to a major college coach. He played well at the clinic. Brown was impressed with Shaq's abilities. He asked Shaq how long he had been a soldier. Brown was surprised to learn that Shaq was only 13 years old.

Shaq began to have troubles off the court. Philip once learned that Shaq had stolen some items out of a car. Philip was very upset with Shaq. He gave Shaq strict rules about where and when he could go out. Shaq did not like Philip's rules at first, but he began using his time at home to practice basketball. His skills continued to improve.

Return to the United States

In 1987, Philip was transferred to a base in Texas. The family again returned to the United States. There, Shaq attended Cole High School near San Antonio. He was in 11th grade.

Cole had a good basketball team. With Shaq, it became even better. The team went 32-1 for the season. Basketball scouts quickly noticed Shaq. Many colleges recruited him to play for their teams after high school.

Shaq wanted to decide on a college before his last year at high school. He made a list of colleges he wanted to consider. The list included Kentucky, UCLA, Indiana, North Carolina, and Duke. Shaq also remembered Dale Brown from LSU. Brown had been the first coach to show an interest in Shaq. LSU was not as successful as many of the other colleges Shaq considered. But Shaq decided that he would be happy playing for Brown. Shaq decided to attend LSU.

Shaq enjoyed his final high school season. He led Cole's basketball team to an undefeated record and the state championship. Shaq averaged 32 points, 22 rebounds, and eight blocked shots per game. He also was named the MVP during two national high school All-Star games.

SHAQ'S GROWTH CHART

7 feet
(213 centimeters)

6 feet
(183 centimeters)

5 feet
(152 centimeters)

4 feet
(122 centimeters)

3 feet
(91 centimeters)

2 feet
(61 centimeters)

1 foot
(30 centimeters)

Age 21
7 feet, 1 inches
(216 centimeters)

Age 16
6 feet, 7 inches
(201 centimeters)

Age 12
5 feet, 10 inches
(178 centimeters)

Age 10
5 feet, 3 inches
(160 centimeters)

Age 8
4 feet, 8.5 inches
(144 centimeters)

Age 6
4 feet, 3.5 inches
(131 centimeters)

Age 4
3 feet, 10 inches
(117 centimeters)

CHAPTER 3

College Star

Shaq left home for LSU in the fall of 1989. College life was a big change for him. He was used to life at army bases. His parents had given him strict rules to follow. Shaq enjoyed his new freedom. He was eager to start his college basketball career.

First Year

Many college basketball experts expected the LSU Tigers to have a good season during Shaq's first year. The team's star player was Chris Jackson. Jackson was among the best college guards in the United States. Experts

Shaq joined the LSU Tigers in 1989.

College basketball experts knew that Shaq had the talent to play in the NBA someday.

believed that Shaq would help Jackson make LSU a great team.

Shaq's first game was November 15 against Southern Mississippi. He scored 10 points and grabbed 5 rebounds. LSU won the game 91-80.

Shaq went on to play every game that season. He scored a season-high 26 points in

I'll probably never shoot 80 or 90 percent, because I'm not a shooter, I've never been a shooter. I think what's going on now is I'm just saying to myself, 'Hit them all now.'
—Shaquille O'Neal, Press Conference, 6/15/01

his fourth game. Later, he had 24 rebounds in one game. But he often committed too many fouls. Brown had to take Shaq out of some games to prevent him from fouling out. Shaq also had trouble making free throws. Other players learned to foul him frequently.

The Tigers finished the regular season with a 21-10 record. They earned a spot in the NCAA Tournament. Shaq had 12 points and 11 rebounds in LSU's first tournament game. The Tigers beat Villanova 70-63. They then lost to Georgia Tech 94-91. LSU's season was over.

Breakout Season

Jackson moved on to the NBA after the 1989–90 season. Shaq knew that he had to become the team's star player.

The Tigers lost the first game of the 1990–91 season to Villanova. But they then won six games in a row. One of the wins came against second-ranked Arizona. Shaq scored 29 points and had 14 rebounds during that game.

Later in the season, he scored 53 points in a game against Arkansas State.

On January 26, 1991, Shaq and the Tigers played Florida. Shaq scored 31 points, grabbed 21 rebounds, and blocked 10 shots in the game. It was Shaq's first triple-double. The Tigers won the game 76-66.

Shaq broke his leg late in the season. The Tigers did not play well without him. They lost two important games in a row. But their 20-9 record was still good enough to earn them a spot in the NCAA Tournament. Their first-round game was against Connecticut.

Shaq knew the Tigers had little chance of winning without him in the game. He told Brown that he wanted to play, even though his leg was not fully healed. Shaq scored 27 points and had 16 rebounds in the game. But his effort was not enough. The Tigers lost 79-62.

Shaq had averaged more than 27 points and 14 rebounds per game during the season. Almost every major sports publication named

Shaq was one of the best college players in the United States.

Shaq left college early. He later returned to school so he could graduate.

him the top player in college basketball. Shaq knew he could make millions of dollars if he left LSU to play in the NBA. But he enjoyed college. He wanted to stay one more year.

Final Season
Shaq did not have as much fun during his third year at LSU. Opposing teams had learned to double-team or triple-team Shaq. They fouled

him frequently. The Tigers began the season 3-3. But they then won 11 of their next 12 games. They finished the regular season with a 20-9 record and advanced to the NCAA Tournament.

LSU's first game was against Brigham Young. Shaq set an NCAA Tournament record with 12 blocked shots in the game. The Tigers won 94-83.

The Tigers met the Indiana Hoosiers in the second round. Shaq wanted to have a great game against the Hoosiers. Indiana was one of the schools he had considered attending. He scored 36 points and had 12 rebounds in the game. But Indiana beat the Tigers 89-79.

Shaq had a press conference a few weeks later. He said that college basketball was no longer fun for him. He announced that he would make himself available for the 1992 NBA Draft.

CHAPTER 4

The NBA

The Orlando Magic selected Shaq with the first pick in the 1992 NBA Draft. The Magic had begun playing in the league only two years earlier. The Magic wanted to build the team around Shaq.

Shaq signed a contract with the Magic. It was worth about $40 million over seven years. Shaq also signed an endorsement deal with Reebok that was worth about $20 million. He was ready to play and prove he was worth all of the money he was earning.

The Orlando Magic selected Shaq with the first pick in the 1992 NBA Draft.

Rookie of the Year

Most NBA experts agreed that Shaq could one day become a great NBA player. But not everyone thought that he could do well right away. Shaq quickly proved that he could. He averaged 23.4 points, 13.9 rebounds, and 3.5 blocked shots per game in his rookie year. He also became the first rookie since Michael Jordan to start in an All-Star Game.

One of Shaq's most memorable games came against the Phoenix Suns in February 1993. Shaq got the ball and went up for a dunk. He slammed the ball through the rim and held on for a moment. Suddenly, the backboard shattered into hundreds of pieces. Shaq had torn the rim off. The game stopped for more than 30 minutes while officials replaced the backboard.

The Magic ended the 1992–93 season with a record of 41-41. The team barely missed the playoffs. In just one season with Shaq, the team had improved its record by 20 wins. After the season, Shaq was named the NBA's Rookie of the Year.

Shaq's strength and size made him one of the NBA's best centers.

The Playoffs

Shaq played even better in the 1993–94 season. He averaged 29.3 points per game. The Magic also improved. They won 50 games and advanced to the playoffs.

The Magic played the Indiana Pacers in the first round of the playoffs. The Pacers were a good team with experienced players. They

played good defense against Shaq. He averaged only 20.7 points per game in the series. The Pacers won three straight games to knock the Magic out of the playoffs.

The 1994–95 season was Shaq's best with the Magic. He led the NBA in scoring with 29.3 points per game. During the regular season, the Magic won 57 games. Their success continued in the playoffs. They beat the Boston Celtics in the first round and the Chicago Bulls in the second round. They then beat the Pacers to advance to the NBA Finals.

The Magic's opponent in the Finals was the Houston Rockets. Shaq averaged 28 points per game in the series. But the Rockets won all four games to claim the championship.

The Magic reached the playoffs again in the 1995–96 season. But they lost to the Bulls in the third round. The Bulls swept the Magic in four games. Shaq's NBA season was over, but he was able to continue to play basketball that year. Shaq was on the U.S. men's basketball

Shaq led the Magic to the NBA Finals in 1995.

team that competed in the 1996 Olympics in Atlanta, Georgia. Shaq and the U.S. team easily won the Olympic gold medal.

Making a Change

Shaq was not completely happy in Orlando. His contract with the Magic included an option. He could choose to end his contract after four years. Shaq decided he would like to play for another team. He told Magic officials that he wanted to get out of his contract.

Many teams wanted to sign Shaq. But Shaq knew which team he wanted to join. He signed a seven-year contract with the Los Angeles Lakers. The contract was worth $121 million. It was the biggest contract in NBA history.

Shaq helped the Lakers right away. The Lakers went 56-26 during his first year with the team. It was their best record in six years. They defeated the Portland Trailblazers in the first round of the playoffs. The Utah Jazz beat the Lakers in the second round, 4-1.

The 1997–98 season was even better for Shaq and the Lakers. Shaq averaged

Shaq helped the U.S. men's basketball team win the gold medal at the 1996 Olympics.

28.3 points and 11.4 rebounds per game. The Lakers won 61 regular season games and won their first two playoff series. But the Jazz swept them in the third round.

Shaq averaged 26.3 points per game the following season. The Lakers again advanced to the playoffs. They beat the Rockets in the first round. But the San Antonio Spurs swept the Lakers in the second round. It was the fifth time in six years that Shaq's team had been swept out of the playoffs.

NBA Champions

In the 1999–2000 season, the Lakers had a 67-15 record. Shaq averaged 29.7 points and 13.6 rebounds per game. He scored 61 points in one game against the Los Angeles Clippers. His great season earned him the NBA MVP award.

The Lakers beat the Sacramento Kings and the Phoenix Suns in the first two rounds of the playoffs. They then faced the Trailblazers in the Western Conference Finals. The teams were evenly matched. The series was tied 3-3 entering the final game. The Trailblazers led the Lakers by 15 points early in the fourth quarter. The Lakers then outscored the Trailblazers 25-5 in the final minutes. They won the game and advanced to the NBA Finals.

The Lakers faced the Pacers in the Finals. Shaq scored 43 points and grabbed

In 2000, the Lakers beat the Trailblazers in the Western Conference Finals.

Shaq was named the 2000 NBA Finals MVP after the Lakers defeated the Pacers.

19 rebounds in the first game. The Lakers won the game 104-87.

The Pacers fouled Shaq often in the second game. Shaq is not a good free throw shooter. He usually makes only about half of his free throws. The Pacers wanted to force Shaq to score from the free throw line. Some people called this the "Hack-a-Shaq" defense. Shaq shot a record 39 free throws in the game. He made 18 of them. He finished the game with 43 points and 19 rebounds. The Lakers won the game 111-104.

The Pacers won the third game 100-91. In the fourth game, Shaq fouled out in overtime. Laker guard Kobe Bryant made three important baskets at the end to give the Lakers the win. The Lakers did not play well in the fifth game. The Pacers won by more than 30 points. But the Lakers still led the series 3-2. They needed one more win for the championship.

Shaq scored 41 points and had 12 rebounds in the sixth game. His performance helped the Lakers to a 116-111 victory. The Lakers were the NBA champions. In the six games, Shaq averaged 38 points and almost 17 rebounds per game. He was named the NBA Finals MVP.

CHAPTER 5

Shaquille O'Neal Today

Shaq remains one of the best players in the NBA today. Almost all NBA experts agree that he is the best center in the game. Many people think that he also is the best player.

Another Title

Shaq and the Lakers had another great season in 2000–01. Shaq averaged 28.7 points and 12.7 rebounds per game. Many NBA players and coaches thought that he deserved the NBA MVP award again. But the 76ers' Allen Iverson won the award instead.

Shaq remains one of the best players in the NBA today.

The Lakers advanced to the playoffs and won their first 11 playoff games. They lost only one game in the entire playoffs, for a record of 15-1. Their playoff record was the best in NBA history. They easily won the championship. Shaq again was named NBA Finals MVP.

Shaq and the Lakers have a contract through 2006. Kobe Bryant also has a long contract with the Lakers. Many NBA experts believe the two stars could lead the Lakers to many more championships.

Off the Court

Shaq enjoys spending time with friends and family when he is not playing basketball. He especially likes to spend time with his daughter, Taahirah. She was born in 1996.

Shaq also enjoys spending time with his fans. Shaq Paq is a group he started that allows children in Los Angeles to come to Lakers games and meet Shaq. Shaq also hosts an event called "Shaqsgiving." On Thanksgiving Day, he

Shaq enjoys spending time with his daughter, Taahirah.

buys food and helps serve it to homeless people. During the Christmas season, Shaq dresses up as "Shaq-a-Claus" and brings gifts to children in hospitals.

Shaq also donates millions of dollars each year to charities. He knows that his basketball skills have made him very successful. He hopes his success can help others as well.

Career Highlights

1972—Shaq is born March 6 in Newark, New Jersey.

1989—Shaq's Cole High School team goes undefeated and wins the Texas State Championship; Shaq begins his college career at LSU.

1991—Shaq averages more than 27 points per game for LSU; he is named college basketball Player of the Year by almost every major sports publication.

1992—Shaq is selected by the Orlando Magic with the first pick in the NBA Draft.

1993—Shaq becomes the first rookie since Michael Jordan to start in an NBA All-Star Game; he averages 23.4 points per game and is named NBA Rookie of the Year.

1995—Shaq and the Magic lose to the Houston Rockets in the NBA Finals.

1996—Shaq wins an Olympic gold medal; he signs a seven-year contract with the Los Angeles Lakers.

2000—Shaq leads the Lakers to the NBA Finals victory over the Indiana Pacers; he is named NBA MVP and NBA Finals MVP.

2001—The Lakers defeat the Philadelphia 76ers in the NBA Finals; Shaq is again named NBA Finals MVP.

Words to Know

contract (KON-trakt)—an agreement between an owner and a player; contracts determine players' salaries.

endorse (en-DORSS)—to sponsor a product by appearing in advertisements

option (OP-shuhn)—a part of a contract that allows one side to make a decision without asking the other side; Shaquille O'Neal had an option in his contract with the Orlando Magic that allowed him to leave the team after four years.

recruit (ri-KROOT)—to try to convince someone to join a group; college basketball coaches recruit high school players to play on their teams.

rookie (RUK-ee)—a first-year player

To Learn More

Bradshaw, Douglas. *Shaquille O'Neal: Man of Steel.* All Aboard Reading. New York: Grosset & Dunlap, 2001.

Dougherty, Terri. *Shaquille O'Neal.* Jam Session. Edina, Minn.: Abdo Publishing, 2001.

Goodman, Michael E. *Shaquille O'Neal.* Mankato, Minn.: Creative Paperbacks, 2001.

Temple, Bob. *Shaquille O'Neal.* Sports Superstars. Chanhassen, Minn.: Child's World, 2001.

Useful Addresses

Basketball Hall of Fame
1150 West Columbus Avenue
Springfield, MA 01105

The National Basketball Association
645 Fifth Avenue
New York, NY 10022

Shaquille O'Neal
c/o The Los Angeles Lakers
Staples Center
1111 South Figueroa Street
Los Angeles, CA 90015

Internet Sites

CNNsi.com—Shaquille O'Neal
http://sportsillustrated.cnn.com/basketball/nba/
   players/847

The Los Angeles Lakers
http://www.nba.com/lakers

Shaquille O'Neal
http://www.shaq.com

Index